eat.shop boston 2nd edition

an encapsulated view of the most interesting, inspired and authentic
locally owned eating and shopping establishments in boston, massachusetts

researched, photographed and written by anna h. blessing
cabazon books : 2009

table of contents

eat

shop

anna's notes on boston

We like to update these guides every two years, but because there is so much gosh-darn eating and shopping to do in this world, a full three years lapsed before I got to eat and shop my way through Boston again for the second edition.

A lot can happen in a city during three years, and this town is no exception. A few notable changes: the T went entirely from tokens to Charlie Cards. The new Institute of Contemporary Art opened (ICA). The transformation of a dilapidated old prison to a shining new hotel, The Liberty, took place. A whole new area of shops and eats popped up in Fort Point channel. Barbara Lynch's food-lovers kingdom multiplied. Rachel and Alon went from having just tiny *Rachel's Kitchen* to opening one of the best restaurants in town: *Hungry Mother*. And *Bodega* is no longer a secret.

A lot, too, has stayed the same. Driving is still nuts. The Boston Common is still the Boston Common. *Christina's Ice Cream* is still the best in town. At *eat.shop*, we love both the changing and the unchanged, the reliable bits and pieces that give a city its personality and the new ones that help to keep things evolving. I hope this second edition of *eat.shop boston* reminds you of familiar favorites and introduces you to new finds.

Outside of the world of eating and shopping, here are a few of my favorite things in Boston:

1 > *ICA*: Views of the harbor from a sharp new building hosting contemporary art exhibitions.

2 > *Harpoon Brewery*: Now offering tours and tastings, and of course, growlers to go.

3 > *The Children's Museum*: A major renovation led to this LEED-certified museum along the Fort Point channel. Don't miss the recycle shop!

4 > *Boston Public Garden*: Host a picnic or make way for ducklings here.

5 > *Isabella Stewart Gardner Museum*: Works by Rembrandt, John Singer Sargent and more, all on display in this lovely building.

about eat.shop

• If you would like the complete regional experience, pick up the brand new *eat.shop new england* as a companion to this book.

• All of the businesses featured in this book are locally owned and operated. In deciding which businesses to feature, we require this criteria first and foremost. Then we look for businesses that strike us as utterly authentic, and uniquely conceived, whether they be new or old, chic or funky. We are not an advertorial guide, therefore businesses do not pay to be featured.

• The maps in this guide are not highly detailed but instead are representational of each area noted. We suggest, if you are visiting, to also have a more detailed map. Streetwise Maps are always a good bet, and are easy to fold up and take along with you. Explore from neighborhood to neighborhood. Note that almost every neighborhood featured has dozens of great stores and restaurants other than our favorites listed in this book. We also have a Google map of Boston with the indicators of the businesses noted at: http://tiny.cc/aowZj. Paste this into the browser of your smart phone, it's quite useful.

• Make sure to double check the hours of the business before you go by calling or visiting its website. Often the businesses change their hours seasonally. The pictures and descriptions of each business are representational—please don't be distraught when the business no longer carries or is not serving something you saw or read about in the guide.

• Small local businesses have always had to work that much harder to keep their heads above water. During these rough economic times, many will close. We apologize if some of the businesses featured here are no longer open. The more you visit the businesses in this book, the better chance they have at staying open.

• The *eat.shop* clan consists of a small crew of creative types who travel extensively and have dedicated themselves to great eating and interesting shopping around the world. Each of these people writes, photographs and researches his or her own books, and though they sometimes do not live in the city of the book they author, they draw from a vast network of local sources to deepen the well of information used to create the guides.

• Please support the indie bookstores in Boston. To find these bookstores, use this great source: www.indiebound.org/indie-store-finder.

• *eat.shop* supports the *3/50 project* (www.the350project.net) and in honor of it have begun our own challenge (please see the back inside cover of this book).

• There are three ranges of prices noted for restaurants, $ = cheap, $$ = medium, $$$ = expensive

previous edition businesses

eat

aquitaine
audobon circle
beacon hill chocolates
b & g oysters
brix
casa romero
central kitchen
cuchi cuchi
franklin cafe
hi-rise bread compay
lulu's bake shoppe
monica's mercato
no. 9 park
olé
oho republique
picco
pigalle
sorriso
teatro
terramia
trattoria di monica
twentyeight degrees
union bar and grille

shop

aunt sadie's
barefoot books
bliss
buckaroo's mercantile
bump
french dressing
johnny cupcakes
luna boston
magpie
mint julep
moxie
parlor
pixie stix
queen bee
stil
the red wagon
the ruby door
turtle
uniform
whim wish

if a previous edition business does not appear on this list, it is either featured again in this edition, has closed or no longer meets our criteria or standards.

a master pdf of the spreads from the previous edition of *eat.shop boston* is available for download

where to lay your weary head

there are many great places to stay in boston, but here's a few of my picks:

liberty hotel
215 charles street
617.224.4000 / libertyhotel.com
standard double from $300
restaurants: clink, scampo
bars: alibi, liberty bar
notes: century old prison turned swank lodging

beacon hill hotel and bistro
25 charles street
617.723.1133 / beaconhillhotel.com
standard double from $250
restaurant: beacon hill bistro
notes: quaint and cozy lodging in the heart of beacon hill

nine zero
90 tremont street
617.772.5800 / ninezero.com
standard double from $260
restaurant: ko prime
notes: stylish comfort in the heart of downtown

xv beacon
15 beacon street
617.670.1500 / xvbeacon.com
standard double from $295
restaurant: mooo....
notes: elegant hotel adjacent to boston common

other lodging options > w hotel (100 stuart street), **omni parker house** (60 school street),
millennium bostonian hotel (26 north street at fanuiel hall)

notes

antico forno

italian country cooking

93 salem street. between cross and prince. green / orange lines: haymarket
617.723.6733 www.anticofornoboston.com
mon - thu 11:30a - 10p fri - sat 11:30a - 10:30p sun 11:30a - 10p

opened in 1992. owners: carla gomes chef: salvatore gollo
$$: all major credit cards accepted
lunch. dinner. reservations recommended

north end >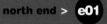

I've heard a few grumbles about preferring *Antico Forno* when it was a small little slip of a restaurant, pre-expansion. What I will say is that it simply does not matter the size or space of this restaurant, the flavor and the portions of the food are big, and that's why you come here. The surroundings seem to melt away as enormous helpings of oven-baked eggplant, pasta and pizza are brought to you from the fiery furnace. You may be surprised to learn that the wood-burning oven used here is a rarity in Boston, which might explain the need to make room for the crowds.

---

imbibe / devour:
04 feotto dello jato nero d'avola
04 alois lageder pinot bianco
ribollita soup
involtini de melanzane
margherita pizza
gnoccchi di patate
rigatoni alla boscaiola
homemade tiramisu

baraka cafe

north african food

80 1/2 pearl street. between auburn and cottage. red line: central square
617.868.3951 www.barakacafe.com
lunch tue - sat 11:30a - 3p dinner tue - sun 5:30 - 10p

opened in 1998. chef / owners: alia rejeb and karim dahim
$ - $$: cash
lunch. dinner. first come, first served

central square >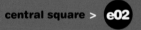

Once in awhile I find myself somewhere in my own town that makes me feel like I'm someplace else. Bostonians, if you're looking for an experience like this, you might want to hop the train to Central Square and walk down the side streets to *Baraka Café*. You will no longer feel like you're in Boston, but instead beamed somewhere far away across the vast ocean. Luckily it doesn't take as long to get to *Baraka* from most places in town, because you'll want to return soon for more cherbat and homemade Berber bread.

imbibe / devour:
cherbat (rose lemonade)
turkish coffee with cardamom
h'rissa tapanade
mahdjouba djazairia
homemade merguez on flat berber bread
zaatar coco
pommes frites
seven spice flourless chocolate torte

beacon hill hotel & bistro

a bistro for travelers and locals alike

25 charles street. corner of chestnut. red line: charles/mgh
617.723.7575 www.beaconhillhotel.com
see hours on website

opened in 2000. owners: peter and cecilia rait   chef: jason bond
$$ - $$$: all major credit cards accepted
breakfast. lunch. dinner. brunch. reservations recommended

beacon hill > **e03**

While I haven't totally glommed on to the term "stay-cation," I do think it's worth reassessing your own city as a place to explore and enjoy as much as a far-away destination. Take the *Beacon Hill Hotel and Bistro,* for example. How many times have you walked by and gazed in to see the relaxed patrons sitting in a window seat, enjoying a morning repast or a cozy evening meal? Locals, don't let the out-of-towners have all of the fun—this bistro and bar is for staycationers and vacationers alike.

imbibe / devour:
loimer lois grüner veltliner
pierre sparr red silk pinot noir
confit duck leg with grits & collard greens
housemade charcuterie
skate wing with brown butter hazelnuts
yorkshire pork shoulder with cider raisin sauce
housemade cavatelli, braised chicken & bacon
sauternes poached pears over vanilla risotto

bin 26 enoteca

restaurant and wine bar with a seasonally-driven menu

26 charles street. corner of chestnut. red line: charles/mgh

617.723.5939 www.bin26.com

mon - thu noon - 10p fri noon - 11p sat 11a - 11p sun 11a - 10p

opened in 2006. owner: babak bina chef / owner: azita babak

$$: all major credit cards accepted

lunch. dinner. reservations recommended

beacon hill >  **e04**

I've just been to my dentist, and it turns out I'm a grinder and a clencher. No wonder, who sleeps peacefully these days? More than ever there is a need for a glass of wine, and thus, one needs a great place to have one. I'm pretty sure that a regular trip to *Bin 26* would cut back on my trips to the dentist. And where before I indulged in a glass of red wine for my medical health, I'll now have a second for my dental health. So let's raise a glass, to good dental, medical and mental health, and to *Bin 26*, for giving us an alternative to going to the doctor.

imbibe / devour:
06 clos la coutale cahors malbec
02 triacca 'la gatta' riserva nebbiolo
roasted golden & red beet & endive salad
beef carpaccio with aged parmesan & arugula
hanger steak with roasted fingerling potatoes
pan roasted monkfish with chickpea puree
selection of cheeses & salumi
spiced chocolate cake with blood orange sorbet

15

cambridge 1

streamlined pizza joint

c: 27 church street. between brattle and massachussetts. red line: harvard square
f: 1381 boylston street. corner of kilmarnock. green line d: fenway
c: 617.576.1111 / f: 617.437.1111 www.cambridge1.us
daily 11:30a - midnight

opened in 2002. owners: matthew curtis and chris lutes
$$: all major credit cards accepted
lunch. dinner. beer/wine only. first come, first served

harvard square / fenway > **e05**

We are over-stimulated constantly, with a gazillion choices to make, hundreds of things to keep up on, blogs to read, ideas to tweet, texts to type, and plain old electronic mail to send. After all this, I find myself craving an uncluttered atmosphere, and *Cambridge 1* is the ultimate in uncluttered. Even the pizzas are simply numbered, cutting back on wordiness. Choices are edited down, thus decision-making is kept to a minimum, and time is left to sit back and enjoy and relax—it's like being in a vacuum of non-busy-ness. Now I just have to send a quick tweet...

imbibe / devour:
brooklyn lager, harpoon ufo draft
magic hat #9
bresaola, arugula, parmigiano, olive oil & lemon
charcoal grilled pizza:
   1: tomato, fontina, romano, garlic & basil
   5: potato, fontina, parmigiano, rosemary
   10: main lobster, corn, scallion & parmigiano
toscanini's tiramisu ice cream

chocolee chocolates

handmade chocolates

83 pembroke street. between tremont and columbus. orange line: back bay
617.236.0606 www.chocoleechocolates.com
tue - sat 11a - 7p sun 11a - 6p

opened in 2008. owner: lee napoli
$: all major credit cards accepted
treats. first come, first served

south end >  **e06**

My tastes in chocolate have evolved over the years. My first love was a simple, satisfying Hershey bar. But when I was introduced to the cocoa-rich varieties of French and Belgian dark chocolates, my feelings for Hershey's became a thing of the past. Then I discovered the chocolates at *Chocolee Chocolates*. Oh my. Lee enriches and spices truffles in an eye-and-mouth opening way. I'm pretty sure that regressing backwards to my basic chocolate origins would be about as easy as going back to life with non-opposable thumbs.

imbibe / devour:
chocolate beignets made to order
chocolate eclairs filled to order
almond bark
truffles:
  salted caramel
  lavender
  peanut butter with ganache

19

christina's ice cream

homemade ice cream and spices and specialty foods

1255 cambridge street. between prospect and oak. red line: central square
617.492.7021 www.christinasicecream.com
mon - thu 11:30a - 11p fri - sat 11:30a - 11:30p
spice store: mon - fri 10a - 6p sat - sun 11a - 6p

opened in 1983. owner: raymond l. ford
$: cash
treats. first come, first served

When I was working on the first edition of *eat.shop boston* a couple of years back, I made it a point to sample each and every local ice cream shop in town—and I found that my favorite, *Christina's*, blew the other competitors away. I am happy to say that over the years, *Christina's* still reigns supreme in my opinion. And what makes the experience even better is that you can pop into the spice and specialty foods section next door, stock up on a vast selection of spices, and attempt to craft your own ice cream at home—but more likely you'll end up coming back for the goodness here.

imbibe / devour:
ice cream:
  adzuki bean
  kafir lime leaf
  black raspberry
  burnt sugar
  nietzsche's chocolate ascension
  fig pecan
amazing selection of spices

clear flour bakery

best bread in town

178 thorndike street. corner of hamilton. green line b: packard's corner
617.739.0060 www.clearflourbread.com
mon - fri 8a - 8p sat - sun 9a - 7p

opened in 1983. owners: christy timon and abe faber
$: mc. visa
bakery. first come, first served

When the Dutch artist Vermeer died, he owed the bakery in Delft an enormous debt, because his large household ate 8,000 pounds of bread over three years, averaging about ½ pound of bread per person per day. Half a pound per day! You might think, that's far more bread than anyone could reasonably eat. You'll likely be singing a different tune, however, once you come to *Clear Flour Bread*. Here you will understand how you could easily consume at least a pound of bread a day and develop a hefty bread debt. Just be sure to pay your bills here.

imbibe / devour:
breads:
  german rye
  rustic italian
  seeded seven grain
  paris night
  sunshine focaccia
rustic fruit tarts
morning buns

drink

handcrafted cocktails

348 congress street. corner of thompson. red line: south station
617.695.1806 www.drinkfortpoint.com
sun - sat 4p - 1a

opened in 2008. owner: barbara lynch
$$: all major credit cards accepted
snacks. full bar. first come, first served

fort point > **e09**

Do you ever get the sense that somewhere out there, there is a cocktail that was designed just for you? A libation that is exactly what you want? At *Drink*, there's a very good chance that the mixing magicians behind the bar might be able to fulfill your liquor fantasy. Think of this place as the cocktail version of match.com. You give the bartenders some personal information, your likes and dislike—and then they go to work to create the perfect alcoholic chemistry. Be bold and brave. Sidle up to the bar at *Drink* to give it a try. If only dating were so easy.

imbibe / devour:
order anything you desire or:
　fort point cocktail
　'40s style martini
　sazerac
themed canapés like:
　buttermilk biscuits
　bacon wrapped date

east coast grill

bbq and raw bar

1271 cambridge street. between prospect and oak. red line: central square
617.491.6568 www.eastcoastgrill.net
see website for hours

opened in 1985. owner: chris schlesinger chef: patrick spencer
$$ - $$$: all major credit cards accepted
dinner. brunch. first come, first served

inman square > **e10**

In my opinion, there are things worth waiting in line for, and things not worth waiting in line for. Not worth it: the latest iteration of some tickle-me toy, cheesy night clubs, tickets to Britney Spears. Worth it: *East Coast Grill and Raw Bar*. Chances are, when you show up here on any given weekend, you will have a wait ahead of you. But stick it out, grab a beer next door at *Bukowski's*, and consider how happy you will be when you finally get that table, a raw bar platter and some smokey ribs. You can't argue that this is something worth waiting for.

imbibe / devour:
seasonal margarita
loimer gruner veltliner
1/2 dozen oysters
essential raw bar platter
extremely hot crispy hell bone
coriander grilled atlantic swordfish
memphis style dry rubbed pork spare ribs
eastern n.carolina shredded pork sandwich

eldo cake house

chinese bakery

38 harrison avenue. between essex and kneeland. orange line: chinatown
617.350.7977
daily 7a - 7p

opened in 1985. owner: raymond kwong
$: all major credit cards accepted
treats. first come, first served

chinatown > **e11**

My friend, publisher and *eat.shop* grand dame Kaie, sent me a link to the Yelp review for *Eldo Cake House* and told me to check it out. My first thought was, "Holy cow! Never had I read this many rave reviews on a place (and believe me, I read a lot of reviews)." My second thought was, "This place will never live up to the hype," as I tend to take Yelp reviews with a grain of salt. Boy was I wrong. After eating a pineapple bao, a slice of white fruit cake, and a paper cup filled with sponge cake, I was in refined white flour heaven and ready to Yelp along with the rest of the pack in unified praise for *Eldo Cake House*.

imbibe / devour:
strawberry bubble tea
pineapple bao
sponge cake
strawberry cake
fruit tart
egg tart
flower cake
walnut napoleon

29

flour bakery + cafe

mouth-watering breads, pastries and food

se: 1595 washington street. corner of rutland. silver line: newton
fp: 1595 washington street. at congress. red line: south station
se: 617.267.4300 / fp: 617.338.4333 www.flourbakery.com
see website for hours

opened in 2000. chef / owner: joanne chang
$ - $$: all major credit cards accepted
breakfast. lunch. treats. first come, first served

south end / fort point > **e12**

If *Flour Bakery* hadn't opened a second spot in Fort Point Channel, I think the South End location might have exploded in a crazy mess of butter, sugar, flour and hungry patrons, who pack in by the droves every day, seemingly all day long. No doubt the second spot will soon have lines as long as the original—it's hard to stay away from the sticky buns, old-fashioned sour cream cake and dozens of varieties of cookies. You will find yourself waiting in line here with the rest of the hungry hordes, just hoping the guy in front of you doesn't take the last pop tart.

imbibe / devour:
housemade raspberry selzer
pop tarts
banana bread
old-fashioned sour cream coffee cake
homemade hummus sandwich
curried tuna sandwich
meringue clouds
raspberry crumb bars

gaslight

a french brasserie

560 harrison avenue. at waltham. orange line: new england medical center
617.422.0224 www.gaslight560.com
see website for hours

opened in 2007. owner: the aquitaine group   chef: christopher robins
$$ - $$$: all major credit cards accepted
dinner. brunch. late night. reservations recommended

south end > **e13**

As a professional eater, I will share a bit of advice: all the action is at the bar. If I had my druthers, I might never sit at an actual table. At the bar you get: flawless service (where can your server disappear to, after all?), the inside scoop on the place from the bartender because they always like to chat, and a prime spot for eavesdropping on neighbors. In Boston, I prefer to do my drinking, eating and eavesdropping at *Gaslight*. So I'll plan on seeing you there—though watch what you say, I will probably be listening in.

imbibe / devour:
resistance cocktail
édith piaf cocktail
fondue piemontaise
steak tartare
escargots de bourgogne
croque-monsieur
moules frites
chocolate beignets

hungry mother

southern specialties

233 cardinal medeiros avenue. corner of binney. red line: kendall square
617.499.0090 www.hungrymothercambridge.com
tue - sun 5 - 10p late hours menu until 12:30a

opened in 2008. owners: rachel miller munzer, alon munzer and john kessen
owner / chef: barry maiden
$$ - $$$: all major credit cards accepted
dinner. late night. reservations recommended

kendall square > **e14**

I can credit my husband Shawn with introducing me to sweet tea, banana pudding and boiled peanuts. He spent time living in the South, while I grew up in the West, where they don't serve these culinary marvels. I'm happy to say they are all on the menu at *Hungry Mother*. The highly biased Shawn says this place sits at the top of his favorite places to eat in the country. But after I polished off handfuls of boiled peanuts, my plate of French gnocchi, stolen bites of Shawn's catfish and still licked clean the dish of banana pudding, I will say I'm right there with him.

imbibe / devour:
no.99 cocktail: bartender's choice
ruination ipa
boiled virginia peanuts
cornmeal catfish
french style gnocchi
giannone farm roasted chicken
southern-style cornbread
banana pudding

la verdad taqueria

a taqueria

1 lansdowne street. corner of ipswich. green line: kenmore
617.351.2580 www.laverdadtaqueria.com
see website for hours

opened in 2007. owner: ken oringer chef: brian roche
$$: all major credit cards accepted
lunch. dinner. first come, first served

fenway >

A new trend seen around the country is top-talent chefs opening super casual restaurants, like a sandwich shop, and in Ken Oringer's case, a taqueria. Oringer has become a household name in Boston, a chef who regularly appears on "best of" lists with his work at *Clio*. That he opened *La Verdad*, a stone's throw from Fenway, only wins more points for Ken, since he's knocked it out of the park with this tiny taco spot. Sit inside or take food to go, either way be sure to save room for the buttery, cheesy grilled corn on the cob, which happens to make an ideal ball game treat.

imbibe / devour:
jaritos
margaritas
tacos:
  pastor
  pescado
  chile
churros
grilled corn

marco

simple italian

253 hanover street, 2nd floor. between cross and parameter
orange / green lines: haymarket
617.742.1276 www.marcoboston.com
tue - thu 5 - 10p fri - sat 5 - 10:30p sun 4 - 9:30p

opened in 2005. owners: marc orfaly and lorenzo demonaco chef: marc orfaly
$$ - $$$: all major credit cards accepted
dinner. reservations recommended

north end > **e16**

I am a bit like the Princess and the Pea when it comes to tables in restaurants. Anything too close to the bathroom, or to the swinging kitchen doors, or to the wait station, or too drafty, can drive me—and in turn my dining partners who have to listen to my complaints—totally batty and ruin a meal. Which is part of the reason I am in love with *Marco*. Every table in this intimate upstairs restaurant is a good table. Which makes it all the easier to settle in and enjoy the housemade pasta and antipasto to the fullest.

---

imbibe / devour:
north end cooler
marco fizze
1/2 litro rosso della casa
antipasto di marco
insalata di rucola
orecchiette con salsiccia
rigatoni con polpette di maiale
housemade gelato

metropolis café

a brunch destination

584 tremont street. between union park and upton. orange line: back bay
617.247.2931 www.metropolisboston.com
dinner sun - wed 5:30 - 10p thu - sat 5:30 - 11p brunch sat - sun 9a - 3p

opened in 1995. owners: the aquitaine group chef: seth woods
$$: all major credit cards accepted
dinner. brunch. first come, first served

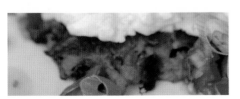

Weekend brunch. I don't have it often, but I love it when I do. But what is the world coming to when you can't find a place that doesn't open before 11am? One recent morning, my husband and I got up and were out in the eerily empty city before 9am. We ended up heading home, bellies still empty, because nothing opened before 11am. Thank goodness for *Metropolis*, where you can start your weekend day early with first things first: a mimosa. Then have the thick-cut cinnamon brioche french toast and the famous grits. All before 9:30am. Beautiful.

imbibe / devour:
grapefruit mimosa
kir royale
house-smoked bacon
griddled blueberry muffin
huevos rancheros
deyve's famous grits
atlantic smoked salmon
thick-cut cinnamon brioche french toast

mike & patty's

a neighborhood sandwich shop

12 church street. corner of fayette. orange line: new england medical center
617.423.3447 www.mikeandpattys.com
tue - fri 7:30a - 3p sat 8a - 2p sun 9a - 2p

opened in 2008. owners: patty sinaiko and mike fitzhenry
$ - $$: mc. visa
breakfast. lunch. treats. first come, first served

bay village > e18

When I heard that Rachel and Alon had closed *Rachel's Kitchen* to pursue a new spot (flip back four pages to *Hungry Mother*), I was excited, but bummed to see the fantastic little corner eatery close. So when *Mike and Patty's* opened up in the space shortly after, continuing in the same vein as *Rachel's*, this was very, very good news. They've more than filled the shoes that *Rachel's Kitchen* left, and have satisfied my cravings with a lovely, gooey grilled banana sandwich. I hope *Mike and Patty's* is here to stay.

imbibe:devour:
mate cascarilla
coffee
grilled banana sandwich
croque monsieur
fried green tomato b.l.t.
bacon & egg, fancy
pulled pork bbq sandwich
verna's doughnuts

myers + chang

tawainese, thai, chinese and vietnamese food

1145 washington street. corner of east berkeley. orange line: n.e. medical center
617.542.5200 www.myersandchang.com
sun - wed 11:30a - 10p thu - sat 11:30a - 11p

opened in 2007. owners: joanne chang and christopher myers chef: matthew barros
$$: all major credit cards accepted
lunch. dinner. reservations recommended

south end > **e19**

Chicken soup for a cold, ginger ale for an upset stomach, and tea and honey for a sore throat—but what to eat when you're just having a crappy, no good sort of day? The nasi goreng bowl of hot steaming goodness at *Myers + Chang* is my suggestion. I'm pretty sure that any funk can be destroyed by this bowl of happiness, but it probably wouldn't hurt to down a mai tai or two to truly elevate your mood. Next time you're in a world of hurt, leave the ice cream in the freezer and get yourself here. Oh, and for those already feeling good? This place can only make things better.

imbibe / devour:
mai tai
asian mojito
edamame & celery slaw
nasi goreng
braised pork belly buns
grilled pork sliders
tea-smoked pork spare ribs
dan dan noodles

neptune oyster

tiny spot for big oysters

63 salem street. corner of cross. orange / green lines: haymarket
617.742.3474 www.neptuneoyster.com
sun - thu 11:30a - 9p (raw bar til 10p) fri - sat 11:30a - 10p (raw bar til 11p)

opened in 2005. owner: jeff nace chef: michael serpa
$$ - $$$: all major credit cards accepted
lunch. dinner. reservations recommended

north end >  **e20**

I say we bring back the boozy lunch and retreat half a century when a plate of oysters and two martinis at lunch was acceptable fare for a mid-week business lunch. Why the heck not? I think going back to work lubricated by a little gin and a lot of oysters might do the body, and the brain, a bit of good in these rough times. I suggest *Neptune Oyster* as the spot for said lunch, but beware—you may well be so enamored that you will find yourself looking to the future by pre-scheduling your next visit to *Neptune* by the end of your meal.

imbibe / devour:
07 aglianico feudi de san gregorio
chenin blan mulder-bosch
clam chowder
neptune plateau from the raw bar
pan-roasted whole mediterranean bronzini
pan-seared main diver scallops
neptune burger
maine lobster roll

oleana

arabic-inspired foods

134 hampshire street. between elm and norfolk. red line: central square
617.661.0505 www.oleanarestaurant.com
sun - thu 5:30 - 10p fri - sat 5:30 - 11p

opened in 2001. chef / owner: ana sortun owner: gary griffin
$$ - $$$: all major credit cards accepted
dinner. reservations recommended

kendall square > **e21**

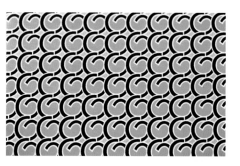

Ever since a recent trip to the Middle East, I have craved certain flavors and spices that I tasted while traveling—several of which I picked up in the spice souks and brought home, hoping to make sense of them and recreate my own Arabic-influenced meals. No such luck, as it turns out. I'm much better at enjoying this cuisine than actually making it. The food at *Oleana* transports me immediately back to the flavors that I so loved, as Ana is a masterful translator. Maybe by eating here I will learn enough to make use of my sad, unused spice collection.

imbibe / devour:
07 samichlaus bier
07 sigalas asirtiko athiri
whipped feta with sweet & hot peppers
spinach falafel with tahini, yogurt, beets & cress
spicy fideos & chick peas with green chard
seared tuna with black olive & almond crumbs
lamb & eggplant dumpling with garlic yogurt
frozen honeycomb souffle with cocoa sherbet

olecito

take-out tacos

12 springfield street. between cambridge and concord. red line: central square
617.876.1374 www.olecito.net
sun - thu 11a - 9p fri - sat 11a - 10p

opened in 2008. chef / owner: erwin ramos
$ - $$: all major credit cards accepted
take out only. first come, first served

inman square > **e22**

I will go to great lengths to avoid visiting the grocery store, even if it means eating such makeshift meals as baked parmesan, celery spread with sun dried tomatoes and cinnamon twists made from old pizza dough. I got this questionable talent from my father, who is known to go for weeks on nothing but pickles and o.j. when he's alone. If you find yourself trying to make a meal from peanut butter and pasta, just get to *Olecito* already. It's just as quick, and a gazillion times better. The time it takes to get totally satisfying, delicious tacos to go: 5 minutes. Not eating p, b+spaghetti for dinner: priceless.

imbibe:devour:
baja taco
carnitas taco
rajas taco
yucateca torta
la milpa torta
chips & guacamole
sonora torta

orinoco kitchen

latin cooking

se: 477 shawmut avenue. corner of concord. orange line: massachusetts avenue
bl: 22 harvard street. between aspinwall and boylston. green line d: brookline village
se: 617.369.7075 / bl: 617.232.9505 www.orinocokitchen.com
see website for hours

opened in 2006. owner: andres branger chef: carlos w. rodriguez
$$: mc. visa
lunch. dinner. brunch. first come, first served

I think this is the test of a truly tasty eating establishment: while in the throes of heavy research, I brunched at five consecutive places one Sunday. Yes, five full meals, one after another, with only the time in between that it takes to walk from one to the next. *Orinoco Kitchen* was the last stop on my list, and one might think that following the four previous feasts, I'd be less than enthused to eat here. But the place is so vibrant, the food so delicious, that it tempts even the full stomach-ed. As I brunched at *Orinoco*, I wondered if I shouldn't come back just hours later for dinner.

imbibe / devour:
papelón con limón jugos
polar cerveza
pernil arepa
verde empanada
tostones
polvorosa de pollo
cordero tradicional
torta fluida

parish cafe

superstar sandwiches from the city's top chefs

361 boylston street. between arlington and berkeley. green line: arlington

617.247.4777 www.parishcafe.com

mon - sat 11:30a - 2a sun noon - 2a

opened in 1992

owners: gordon wilcox, peter culpo, sean and elaine simmons

chef: sean simmons

$$: all major credit cards accepted

lunch. dinner. full bar. first come, first served

You know what would be a really great idea for a restaurant? To get all of the local superstar chefs together and have them all create a signature sandwich for the place—thus creating an extensive, fantastically diverse menu that serves as a cross section of sorts for the city's food scene. Oh wait, *Parish Café* has already done this! I have yet to taste a sandwich from *Parish's* menu that I didn't like, which means that not only does this restaurant rock, but so do all of the chefs that contribute. Long live the sandwich, and long live Boston!

imbibe / devour:
mojito
sandwiches:
  the alternative
  elephant walking on eggs
  the benny
  sean's meatloaf club
  the nebo
  blue ginger

polcari's coffee

coffee and spice market

105 salem street. corner of parameter. orange / green lines: haymarket
617.227.0786 www.northendboston.com/polcaricoffee
mon - fri 9:30a - 6p sat 8:30a - 6p

opened in 1932. owner: bobby eustace
$: cash
grocery. first come, first served

north end > **e25**

When I lived in Rome, I frequented a tiny market where you could find a random assortment of useful things and dry goods that couldn't be found in the nearby Campo dei Fiori market. I loved the smell of this place, and the convenience of it. But mostly I loved the constant influx of locals, chatting about the weather, local gossip and what was new in store. *Polcari's Coffee* is the North End equivalent of that beloved corner market of mine. This is a spot where you feel immediately at home, whether making a weekly trip in for spices or getting some coffee and a little friendly chatter.

imbibe / devour:
coffee:
   colombian supremo
   italian espresso roast
   organic mexican
grains & legumes
spices
nuts

sofra

middle eastern bakery and cafe

1 belmont street. corner of mt. auburn. red line: harvard square
617.661.3161 www.sofrabakery.com
mon - fri 8a - 8p sat 8a - 6p sun 8a - 3p

opened in 2008. owners: ana sortun, gary griffin and maura kilpatrick
$$: all major credit cards accepted
breakfast. lunch. bakery. classes. first come, first served

west cambridge > **e26**

It was while visiting *Sofra* when I realized how truly difficult my job can be. Consider this dilemma: you are in front of the baked goods at *Sofra*, one of the most desirable places to be in all of Boston, and you have to pick what to eat. Do you get the dense, rich and buttery sesame pecan bar? Or a light and airy baked doughnut spiced on top? Or one of the highly lauded fruit tarts? Folks, this is the sort of daily trauma I deal with—thank your lucky stars if you've got a desk job, so you don't have to make such difficult decisions.

imbibe / devour:
housemade chai
rhubarb & mint sharbat
brown butter bread pudding
turkish breakfast
almond rose cake
shashuka
chicken schwarma flatbread
pistachio olive oil cake

south end buttery

a local mainstay

314 shawmut avenue. corner of union park. orange line: back bay
617.482.1015 www.southendbuttery.com
see website for hours

opened in 2006. owners: richard gordon and andrew barker
$$: all major credit cards accepted
breakfast. lunch. dinner. brunch. coffee/tea. first come, first served

south end > e27

If you believe there is a superior substance to butter in this world, by all means please share. And if you know of a better blend than butter, sugar and flour—I'm all ears. The *South End Buttery* proves my point with their cupcakes, cookies and other baked marvels. And though the good people at *South End* no doubt believe there is nothing better than butter, they know that we cannot, alas, subsist on butter alone. So they offer up square meals also, from breakfast to lunch to dinner. But thank goodness, you're never very far from the buttery goodness for dessert.

imbibe / devour:
cappuccino
donut muffin
cupcakes
banana walnut loaf
buttery b.l.t.
turkey chutney sandwich
curried chicken salad sandwich
turkey chili

south end formaggio

specialty food shop

268 shawmut avenue. between milford and waltham. orange line: back bay
617.350.6996 www.southendformaggio.com
mon - fri 9a - 8p sat 9a - 7p sun 11a - 5p

opened in 1985. owners: valerie and ihsan gurdal
$ - $$: all major credit cards accepted
grocery. first come, first served

south end > **e28**

Ihsan and Valerie, the owners of *South End Formaggio*, are great teachers. It's as much fun to read their notes about the spices, cheeses, biodynamic wines, organic beers and chocolates, as it is to actually eat the things. Did you know that smoked Viking sea salt is from the ash of burnt seaweed and was used in the age of the Vikings as payment? Or that the fertile plains of Lodi, Italy, affect the taste of the local butter, which gives La Tortionata Lodi, a rich cake with almonds, its unparalleled deliciousness? So much to learn, so much to taste—this is the fun sort of homework.

imbibe / devour:
smoked viking salt
la tortionata lodi
farrah's butter fudge
amaretti di sant'angelo
elderflower syrup
oil-cured provençal olives
blue ledge farm lake's edge cheese
goat cheese, fig jam & arugula sandwich

sportello

mod italian lunch counter

348 congress street. between farnsworth and thompson. red line: south station
617.737.1234 www.sportelloboston.com
see website for hours

opened in 2008. chef / owner: barbara lynch
$$ - $$$: all major credit cards accepted
lunch. dinner. bakery. reservations recommended

fort point > **e29**

No. 9 Park, *B&G Oysters*, *The Butcher Shop*, *Drink*, and now *Sportello*—Barbara Lynch, how *do* you do it?! I admit, I came to this spot ready to be disappointed, biting my nails and worrying, had Barbara spread herself too thin? Turns out no, because Barbara is Boston's Wonder Woman—and there is no such thing as a superhero spreading herself too thin. And because she is super human, I'd like Barbara to take her powers throughout the world, so that everywhere I go, I will never have to be without a bowl of fresh pasta, hot tomato soup or a perfect cocktail.

imbibe / devour:
06 peter zemmer pinot nero
spicy tomato soup
fennel & celery salad
strozzapreti
papardelle
roasted turnips
chocolate budino
chocolate ginger cake

65

sweet

delightful cupcakes

49 massachusetts avenue. between commonwealth and marlborough
green line: hynes convention/ica
617.247.2253 www.sweetcupcakes.com
mon - tue 11a - 7p wed - sat 11a - 9p sun noon - 7p

opened in 2008. owner: courtney forrester
$ - $$: all major credit cards accepted
treats. first come, first served

back bay >

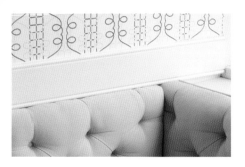

I'm a real sucker for the "something-of-the-month" clubs. I'm a member of several wine clubs, a fruit and vegetable co-op with produce deliveries and even a letterpress card-of-the-month club. It's like having a mini birthday celebration with each delivery. Now if only *Sweet* had a cupcake-of-the-month club, it would really be a celebratory delivery. When it comes to cupcakes, some are sweet, some edgy, some silly and some snooty. I prefer the classic sort, which is what *Sweet* creates. If these *Sweet* treats can't come to me every month, I suppose I'll just have to go to them.

imbibe / devour:
cupcakes:
  organic karat
  red velvet
  dark chocolate
  the sweet cake
  coconut
  mango
  macaroon

67

tatte

fine bakery and coffee shop

1003 beacon street. between st. mary's and carlton. green line c: st. mary's street
617.232.2200 www.tattecookies.com
mon - thu 7a - 8p fri 7a - 10p sat 8a - 10p sun 8:30a - 8p

opened in 2008. owner: tzurit or
$ - $$: all major credit cards accepted
treats. first come, first served

brookline > e31

I am just about positive that Handel's *Halleluiah Chorus* was playing in my head when I set foot in *Tatte* for the first time. I could finally stop searching! I had found my Holy Grail—the most lovely little bakery and café ever, where the café au lait tastes as though they've imported the water, and the warm brioche are served with fresh fruit preserves and butter. To sit with a paper, my coffee and bread and butter—I have no doubt that I could die here happy. But before I do that, I must spread the gospel of the deliciously and aesthetically perfect *Tatte*.

imbibe:devour:
cappuccino
handmade pear juice
brioche & fresh fruit preserves
pecan nutbox
pistachio pie
hazelnut rose
belgian chocolate brioche
animal crackers

ten tables

farm-fresh food

jp: 597 centre street. between pond and lochstead. orange line: green street

wc: 5 craigie circle. at craigie street. red line: harvard square

jp: 617.524.8810 / c: 617.576.5444 www.tentables.net

mon - thu 5:30 - 10p fri - sat 5:30 - 10:30p sun 5 - 9p

opened in 2002. owner: krista kranyak owner / chef: dave punch

$$$: all major credit cards accepted

dinner. reservations recommended

jamaica plain / west cambridge > **e32**

Technically, *Ten Tables* is no longer just ten tables, with the opening of a second location in Cambridge. But do you hear any of these twenty tables complaining? I didn't think so. You'll be far from harping on technical details like this, once you enter either of these little restaurants and call one of the tables your own. It feels a bit like being at a friend's house for dinner, and your friend happens to be a genius at serving seasonally fresh food. On nights when they are especially busy, which is quite often, you might even find yourself wishing for another ten tables, to make room for you and yours.

imbibe / devour:
ten tables "tini"
carafe of house wine
spicy steak tartare
fluke crudo with chives, olive oil, sea salt & citrus
skillet-roasted gianonne chicken
jamon serrano wrapped wild striped bass
housemade boudin blanc
chocolate terrine with thai basil ice cream

the beehive

eclectic eatery and bar

541 tremont street. between berkeley and clarendon. orange line: back bay
617.423.0069 www.beehiveboston.com
daily 5p - 2a. jazz brunch sat - sun 10:30a - 3p

opened in 2007. owners: jack bardy, jennifer epstein, bill keravuori and darryl settles
chef: rebecca newell
$$ - $$$: all major credit cards accepted
lunch. dinner. brunch. reservations recommended

south end > **e33**

As Chef Rebecca debated what to have me photograph at *The Beehive*, she asked a co-worker, "What do you think—the shakshouka—that's hot, yes? What about a burger? Is it too trendy? What do you think?" This might just sum up the vibe at *The Beehive*, perhaps the only place in town that would give the care and consideration to whether a burger was considered too trendy or not. Good thing they decided it wasn't, and I did get to shoot it, because friends, this is one burger you should be in the know about, trendy or otherwise.

imbibe / devour:
sloe gin fizz
la vie en rose cocktail
raw bar platter
baked goat cheese with honey
prosciutto & mozzarella flatbread pizza
grilled tomato & farmhouse cheddar sandwich
the beehive prime burger
cheese & gravy frites

the butcher shop

a butcher shop and restaurant

552 tremont street. corner of waltham. orange line: back bay
617.423.4800 www.thebutchershopboston.com
see website for hours

opened in 2003. owner / chef: barbara lynch
$$$: all major credit cards accepted
lunch. dinner. reservations accepted for parties of six or more

south end > e34

All your gastronomic needs could be met in the space of less than a square city block. First there's *The Butcher Shop,* which offers up a selection of housemade sausages and pâtés, then next door at *Plum Produce* you can pick up fresh produce and a few items you might need for your meal at home, and finally—to ensure your meal truly is tasty—you can enroll in a cooking class at *Stir*. If all of this sounds beyond your scope, then just find yourself a seat at *The Butcher Shop* for lunch or dinner, and let Barbara and her genius staff do all of the work for you.

imbibe / devour:
07 schloss gobelsberger
antipasti della casa
pâtés & terrine
hot dog à la maison
tbs hamburger with onion rings
spicy roasted fingerlings
whole caramelized spanish onion
rhubarb cobbler

the helmand

cuisine from afghanistan

143 first street. corner of bent. green line: lechmere
617.492.4646 www.helmandrestaurantcambridge.com
sun - thu 5 - 10p fri - sat 5 - 11p

opened in 1994. owner: mahmood karzai
$$: all major credit cards accepted
dinner. reservations recommended

kendall square > **e35**

It's easy to say, "Well, this is good, but it doesn't even come close to the amazing paella I had in Sevilla," or "This pasta is good, but it's nothing like the incredible pasta in Italy." You get the point. Chances are, however, few people are going to come to *The Helmand* and expound on their know-it-all, first-hand experience of Afghan cuisine. But after a meal here, you might find yourself, when dining again at a different Afghani restaurant, saying, "Well, it's good, but it's not like they make it at *The Helmand*."

imbibe / devour:
turkish coffee
shor nakhod
kaddo
mantwo
aushak
chowpan
feereney
cardamom & pineapple cake

toro

tapas

1704 washington street. between worcester and springfield
orange line: massachusetts
617.536.4300 www.toro-restaurant.com
see website for hours

opened in 2005. owner: ken and celine oringer   chef: jamie bissonnette
$$ - $$$: all major credit cards accepted
lunch. dinner. brunch. reservations recommended

south end > **e36**

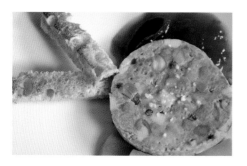

My parents rarely fight, and my mom rarely gets mad. But a few years back my dad infuriated my mom, and she couldn't get over it. He demanded she accept his apology and in order to secure it, and a laugh, he stripped down, marched outside and threatened to circle the front of the house in the buff if she didn't soften. That did the trick, but men, I have a better solution for getting out of the doghouse: take your lovely wife to *T.W. Food*. Husband and wife duo Tim and Bronwyn and will inspire culinary (and marital) love with food that could make the Bickersons get along.

---

imbibe / devour:
06 kamiak cabernet sauvignon
03 dog point chardonnay
local macomber turnip soup
terrine du chef
grass-fed beef
local shelfish quiche
70 minute egg
vanilla panna cotta with darjeeling tea gelée

ula café

café and bakery

284 amory street. between cornwall and boylston. orange line: stony brook
617.524.7890 www.ulacafe.com
mon - fri 7a - 7p sat - sun 8a - 7p

opened in 2007. owners: korinn koslofsky and kate bancroft
$ - $$: all major credit cards accepted
breakfast. lunch. first come, first served

jamaica plain > **e39**

There are times when I must put my life on the line for this job, like when I was shooting pictures of the popovers *Ula Café*. Popovers, you see, are a hot commodity here. They come in small, limited batches, fresh from the oven, immediately snatched up by anxiously awaiting patrons. So when Korinn placed a full fresh batch in front of me to shoot, I could feel those hungry eyes staring at me, ready to pounce! Once you taste one, you'll understand the hungry hordes intense desire—and my subsequent fear to stand in the way of anyone who wanted one.

imbibe / devour:
mem teas
spicy hot chocolate
oatmeal with milk
popovers
sunrise muffin
homemade granola
egg salad sandwich
black forest ham sandwich

verna's

damn-good doughnuts

2344 massachusetts avenue. corner of norris. red line: davis
617.354.4110 www.vernaspastry.com
mon - sat 5:30a - 6p sun 7a - 1p

opened in 1950. owner: richard brunet
$: mc. visa
treats. first come, first served

davis square > **e40**

Boston is a donut town, home of the donut conglomerate *Dunkin' Donuts*, which makes it tough for small, local donut shops to survive. So this means that when a small local donut shop does survive, it's pretty damn good. *Verna's* has been around for more than 30 years now. A few years ago rumors circulated that the beloved donut shop was closing, putting the city in a near panic. Phew—*Verna's* still lives on today, the world can continue turning, and you can continue to load up on these addictive doughnuts for your morning fix.

imbibe / devour:
hot coffee with cream & sugar
doughnuts:
  plain cake
  jelly
  jam-filled
  chocolate glazed
  powdered sugar
  maple bar

volle nolle

a sandwich shop

351 hanover street. between prince and bennet. green / orange lines: haymarket
617.523.0003
mon - sat 11a - 4p

opened in 2006. owners: armando galvao and torri crowell chef: rodolfo gil
$ - $$: all major credit cards accepted
lunch. first come, first served

north end >

Volle Nolle is a sandwich shop where the 'wiches are so good, I wanted to try each and every one, and where the owners are so friendly, they know nearly everyone who walks through the door. But take note, do not, whatever you do, overlook the brownies. This would be a grave error. These brownies are so good, it will make you wonder if they're the mind-altering sort. Of course, the sandwiches will keep me coming back—but the brownies here might have me pounding on the window, begging for more, whether *Volle Nolle* be open or closed.

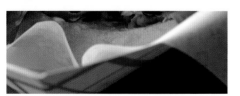

imbibe / devour:
mint iced tea
italian roast coffee
sandwiches:
  cubano
  milanese
  ham & cheese
  portobello
brownies

• back bay

eat

e15 > la verdad taqueria
e24 > parish cafe
e30 > sweet

shop

s5 > bodega
s9 > dress
s17 > kitchen arts
s20 > lester harry's
s23 > matsu
s37> stel's

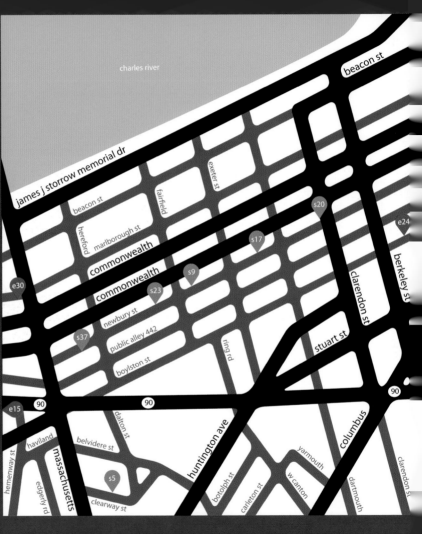

note: all maps face north

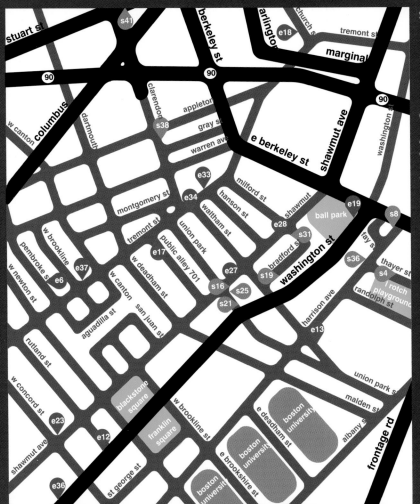

south end ·

eat

e6 > chocolee chocolates
e12 > flour bakery and cafe
(first location)
e13 > gaslight
e17 > metropolis
e18 > mike & patty's
e19 > myers + chang
e23 > orinoco kitchen
e27 > south end buttery
e28 > south end formaggio
e33 > the beehive
e34 > the butcher shop
e36 > toro
e37 > tremont 647

shop

s4 > bobby from boston
s8 > diseño | bos
s16 > hudson
s19 > lekker
s21 > looc
s25 > michelle willey
s31 > polka dog bakery
s36 > simplemente blanco
s38 > tadpole
s41 > urban living studio

note: all maps face north

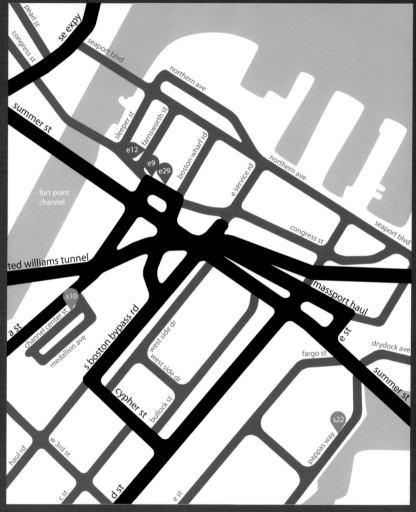

• fort point channel

eat

e9 > drink
e12 > flour bakery and cafe
(2nd location)
e29 > sportello

shop

s10 > front
s22 > machine age

chinatown •

eat
e11 > eldo cake house

shop
s43 > vessel

note: all maps face north

• **north end**

eat

e1 > antico forno
e16 > marco
e20 > neptune oyster
e25 > polcari's coffee
e41 > volle nolle

shop

s2 > acquire
s35 > shake the tree

note: all maps face north

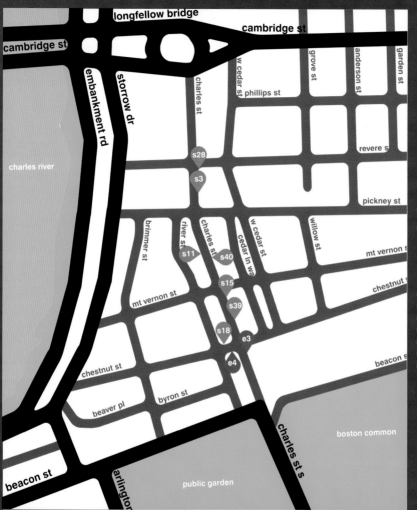

beacon hill ●

eat

e3 > beacon hill hotel and bistro

e4 > bin 26 enoteca

shop

s3 > black ink (1st location)
s11 > good
s15 > holiday
s18 > koo de kir
s28 > north river outfitters
s39 > the beauty mark
s40 > twentieth century limited

note: all maps face north

cambridge

- **kendall square**
- **central square**

eat

e2 > baraka cafe
e14 > hungry mother
e21 > oleana
e35 > the helmand

shop

s26 > nest

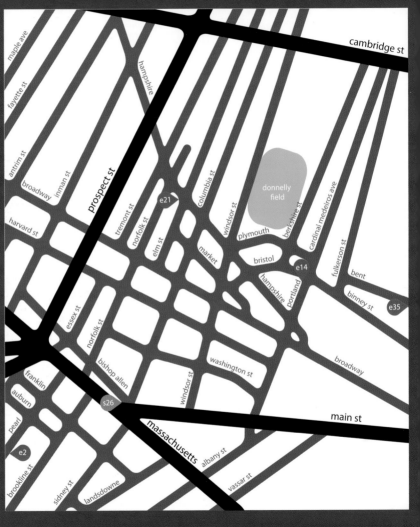

note: all maps face north

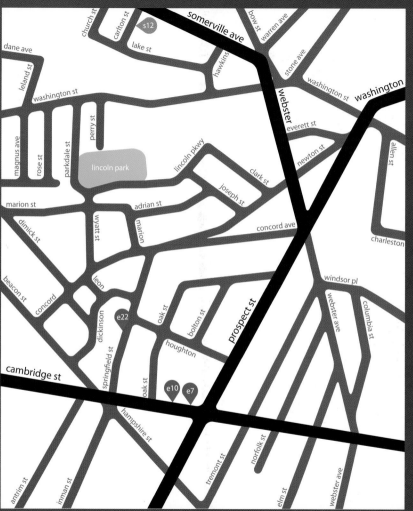

cambridge

inman •
square
sommerville •

eat

e7 > christina's ice cream
e10 > east coast grill and raw bar
e22 > olecito

shop

s12 > grand

note: all maps face north

cambridge

• porter
square

eat

e40 > verna's

shop

s1 > abodeon
s14 > greenward
s27 > nomad

note: all maps face north

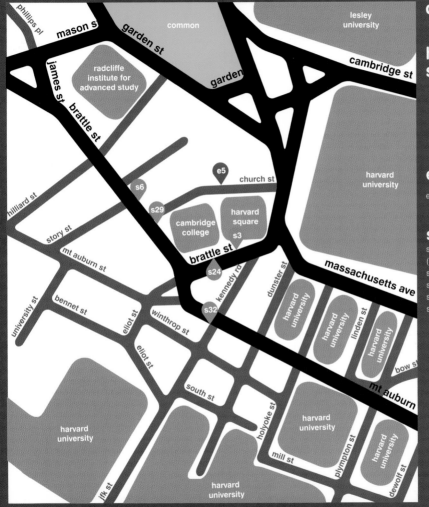

cambridge

harvard square •

eat

e5 > cambridge 1

shop

s3 > black ink
(second location)
s6 > colonial drug
s24 > motto/mdf
s29 > passport
s32 > proletariat

note: all maps face north

• west cambridge

eat

e26 > sofra
e32 > ten tables
(2nd location)
e38 > t.w. food

shop

s13 > graymist studio
s33 > reside

note: all maps face north

brookline •

eat

e8 > clear flour bread
e23 > orinoco kitchen
(2nd location)

e31 > tatte

shop

s30 > pod

note: all maps face north

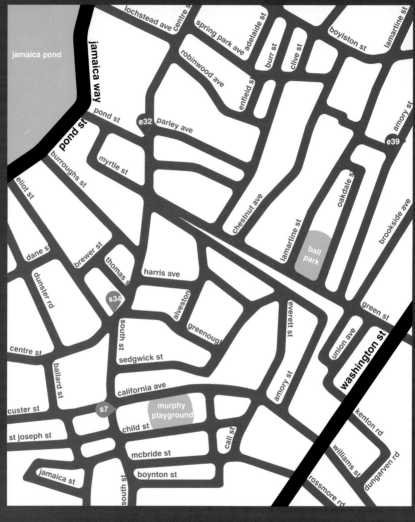

- **jamaica plain**

jamaica pond

jamaica way

pond st

eat
e32 > ten tables
(1st location)
e39 > ula café

shop
s7 > dame
s34 > salmagundi

lochstead ave
centre st
spring park ave
adelaide st
burr st
clive st
boylston st
lamartine st
robinwood ave
enfield st
amory st
pond st
e32 parley ave
e39
burroughs st
myrtle st
ellot st
chestnut ave
lamartine st
oakdale s
brookside ave
dane s
brewer st
thomas s
harris ave
ball park
dunster rd
s34
alveston
greenough
everett st
green st
centre st
south st
sedgwick st
amory st
union ave
washington st
ballard st
california ave
s7
murphy playground
custer st
child st
call st
kenton rd
st joseph st
mcbride st
williams st
dungarven rd
jamaica st
south st
boynton st
crossmore rd

note: all maps face north

notes

abodeon

mid-century modern meets modern day

1731 massachusetts avenue. between garfield and linnaean. red line: porter square

617.497.0137 www.abodeon.com

mon - sat 10a - 6p sun noon - 5p

opened in 1998. owners: dale and terri anderson

all major credit cards accepted

online shopping. wish list

porter square >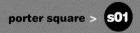

Shopping at *Abodeon* is a bit like time traveling. You'll hop between decades as you browse, from Danish modern pieces to Paul McCobb designs from the '50s, then back earlier to Eva Zeisel's '40s era ceramics, then forward to the current designs of today. It goes on like this throughout the store, which somehow makes complete sense under Dale and Terri's direction. They've created a time capsule of designs from the past century, and all you have to do is pick and choose which decade you prefer or mix it up. Whatever you like.

covet:
bryan parks recycled bamboo chopsticks
paul mccobb '50s desk
wendell smith wood candle holders
kofod larsen chair
krenit salad servers
black walnut coat rack
paul mccobb lamp
danish bowls & servers

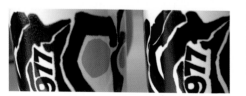

acquire

new and vintage goods

61 salem street. between cross and prince. green / orange lines: haymarket
857.362.7380 www.acquireboutique.com
see website for hours

opened in 2008. owner: nikki g. dalrymple
all major credit cards accepted
online shopping. design services

north end >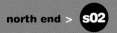

Moving is a good way to take stock of all the things you have acquired throughout the years. I find that pulling items out of your home and seeing, for example, your dingy old chair sitting on the front lawn, makes you realize that a lot of the stuff you've acquired you don't actually want. Moving or not, it's time to come to *Acquire* and fill your home with pieces you do want. I gave myself this talking to while looking around here, and walked away with a Warren Bennet chair, certainly one of the favorite things I've acquired in the last year.

covet:
'60s danish modern wood monkeys
hand-blown wine glasses
ward bennett wicker chair
vintage cordial glasses
convex bullseye mirrors
keep calm tote
galvanized steel console
17th century scandinavian bird print

black ink

odds and ends and unexpected necessities

hs: 5 brattle street. between eliot and church. red line: harvard square
bh: 101 charles street. between revere and pinckney. red line: charles/mgh
hs: 617.497.1221 / bh: 617.723.3883 www.blackinkboston.com
mon - sat 10a - 8p sun 11a - 7p / mon - sat 10a - 7p sun noon - 6p

opened in 1994. owner: susan corcoran
all major credit cards accepted
online shopping

harvard square / beacon hill > s03

WOOD YOU LIKE TO EAT 14.

In order to get me, age 7, to stop crying over my mom's three week trip to Africa, my sister asked me help her write tons of notes to hide in my mom's luggage. She found folded slips of paper all during the trip—in her toiletries, jewelry pouch, her book. Ever since, I've loved surprise notes and memos. Something about *Black Ink* makes me feel the same way. It feels like there are little surprises hidden in every inch of this amazing store, and you want to spend hours exploring. And now instead of little slips of paper, I can buy my mom little presents from here to keep her smiling.

covet:
framing tape
normann copenhagen vippe glasses
porcelain keys
rubber stamp set
scanwood mortar & pestle
writer's block
kokeshi dolls
jumbo jack

bobby from boston

men's and women's vintage clothing
19 thayer street. corner of harrison. orange line: back bay
617.423.9299
tue - sat noon - 6p and by appointment

opened in 1996. owner: bobby garnett
all major credit cards accepted

south end >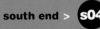

I recently had great success selling on eBay, with an exciting, edge-of-my-seat bidding war, a couple dozen watchers ready to pounce, and in the end, three times the sales that I had anticipated. I wished I had an endless trove of gently used, super desirable things to sell—I marvel at the business that could be brought in. Such is the daily and constant success of Bobby, whose entire store, *Bobby From Boston*, is filled with the best of the past. I would happily sell whatever I had to make room for the amazing pieces that Bobby has here. His loss, my gain.

covet:
striped silk ties
suitcases
overalls
levi's
striped t's
eye glasses
cowboy boots
dress shoes

bodega

secret sneaker shop

6 clearway street. between massachusetts and huntington
green line: hynes convention center/ica
617.421.1550 www.bdgastore.com
mon, wed - sat 11a - 6p sun noon - 5p

opened in 2006. owners: jay gordon, oliver mak and dan n
all major credit cards accepted
online shopping

back bay >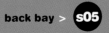

The cat is out of the bag, in a big way, about *Bodega*. A few years ago when I included this spot in the first *eat.shop boston*, this hidden place drew responses like, "Oh yeah, I've heard rumors about that place—where is it and how do you find it?" Now it's gone from being hard to find, to being hard to actually see because of the swaths of people that are continually filling this store. So I don't need to tell you how to find it, but I will tell you that you will want to come and see what the fuss is all about.

covet:
supra stubs skytop
adidas stan smith 80s a.r.c.
kazuki kuraishi for adidas
adidas y-3 black & white striped
air zoom toki lux
puma mid x undefeated 24k collection
white nike af1s
nike sportswear tier0

113

colonial drug

old-world pharmacy and perfume shop

49 brattle street. between appian and church. red line: harvard square
617.864.2222
mon - fri 8a - 7p sat 8a - 6p

opened in 1947. owner: cathy botindari
cash only

harvard square > **s06**

Somewhere along the line, the fantastic pharmacies and apothecaries of old were replaced with mega drugstores where you can buy everything from milk to batteries to shoe polish to Draino. Do you really want to buy your drain cleaner at the same place you buy your perfume? I don't think so. Thankfully a few of the gems from the old world have stayed, and *Colonial Drug* is one of them. Perusing the European apothecary brands and the classic balms and salves here, I risk sounding like my grandparents when I say, "They just don't make 'em like they used to."

covet:
boto toothpaste
yu be moisturizer
thayers slippery elm lozenges
urtekram children's toothpaste
klorane shampoo
col. ichabod conk's mustache wax
horto botanico artichoke soap
talba glycerine soap

dame

fine vintage and independent design

68 south street. between carolina and child. orange line: forest hills
617.935.6971 www.jpdame.com
see website for hours

opened in 2009. owner: dany pearson
all major credit cards accepted

jamaica plain > **s07**

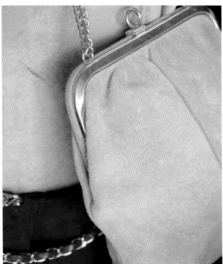

My grandfather recently moved out his condo where he had lived for many decades. We all came to help him move, and in the process, uncovered a closet filled with classic shoes, dresses and hats that had been my grandmother's, or her mother's. All of us Blessing girls tried them on and divvied them up, and we all wished the closet would never end. Because of *Dame*, it doesn't have to. This is like a glorious, extended version of my grandmother's coveted collection, and you'll be happy to know you don't need to be my next of kin to try it all on.

covet:
black & silver sparkly heels
suede pink purse
vintage cufflinks
red & black men's smoking jacket
silk scarves
iridescent heels
vintage trunks

117

diseño | bos

south american style for the home

409 harrison avenue. corner of berkeley. orange line: new england medical center
617.423.2008 www.disenoboston.com
tue - fri noon - 6p sat - sun 11a - 5p

opened in 2007. owner: frank campanale
all major credit cards accepted
online shopping

south end > **s08**

On a recent trip to Buenos Aires, I was near frantic wanting to transport all of the amazing Argentinian textiles, rugs and furniture back home with me. I only made it back with a few rugs and flea market finds, but thanks to Frank and his store, *Diseño*, I now have a North American resource for my South American design cravings. And as I'm always thinking about eating and shopping, Frank noted to me that he has a second home in Buenos Aires, so keep that in mind for any upcoming travel, as he's a trusty guide for the top eats and shops there.

covet:
leather rugs
woven wool pillows
soap from buenos aires
south american music
vintage seltzer bottles
folding chairs with leather & canvas covers
argentinian rugs

dress

a stylish shop for women

221 newbury street. between fairfield and exeter. green line: copley
617.424.7125 www.dressboston.com
mon - thu 11a - 7p fri - sat 11a - 6p sun noon - 5p

opened in 2005. owners: martha hilfinger and jane schlueter
all major credit cards accepted
online shopping

back bay >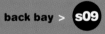

I remember having a favorite corduroy dress when I was a little girl that I never wanted to take off. I wanted to wear it to school every day, to play in, even to sleep in. I only wish I loved most of my clothes that much these days. I have a feeling that I might be just as enamored again if I owned some of the clothing from *Dress*. BFFs Martha and Jane probably also remember that first clothing crush, when they first met as little girls. Now they have filled their store with pieces that you'll likely fall in love with—and even want to sleep in.

covet:
fiorentini + baker boots
philip lim 3.1 belts
shipley & halmos navy dress
adam hot pink dress
vanessa bruno dresses
tucker blouses
vena cava tops
twelfth st. by cynthia vincent pink lace dress

121

front

goods from bob's your uncle
25 channel center street. between binford and iron. red line: south station
857.362.7289 www.bobsyouruncle.com
tue - fri 10a - 6p sat noon - 5

opened in 2008. owner: michele and martin yeeles
all major credit cards accepted
online shopping

fort point >

For anyone who thinks you can't be both practical and fun, meet Martin and Michelle, who put the fun in function—every item in their store, *Front*, is both useful and playful. This talented twosome are the designers of "Bob's Your Uncle," a paper goods and gift line that I have long loved, which can be found in its entirely at *Front*. Here is where you'll find things that make tedious chores like list-making fun with their "too much to do" list pad or their "8 days a week planning journal." Shopping at *Front* is a very responsible activity.

covet:
bobs your uncle:
  to do list
  animal alphabet book
  wrapping paper
  sticky page markers
  orla kiely notepad
  park huas felt cases
  kobo candles

good

a highly covetable store

88 charles street. between pinckney and mt. vernon. red line: charles/mgh
617.722.9200 www.shopatgood.com
mon 11a - 7p sat 10a - 6p sun noon - 5p

opened in 2001. owner: paul niski
all major credit cards accepted
online shopping

beacon hill > **s11**

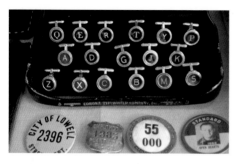

I like to use my art history major to justify my love of shopping. Though I love to explore the sights in any given city, including the museums and the parks, what really excites me is discovering a city's collection of outstanding stores, which are like miniature galleries giving a peak into the world of art and design. My number one spot in Boston to study my type of art? *Good*. I never tire of this tiny shop, where I find something new and unique every time I visit. If only I wanted to attend my early morning art lectures in college as much as I want to come to this store.

covet:
danish pewter i.d. bracelet
antique bracelets
ivory bangles
vintage corkscrews
john derian coasters
horn cups
emily keifer initial necklaces
patch necklaces

grand

grand style for men, women and home

374 somerville avenue. between church and warren. red line: porter square

617.281.6180 www.grandthestore.com

tue - fri noon - 7p sat 11a - 7p sun noon - 6p

opened in 2008. owners: wendy friedman and jon o'toole

all major credit cards accepted

online shopping

somerville > **s12**

In a world of fantastic shops and eateries, it's especially exciting when one such spot opens in a surprising neighborhood, paving the way to what was before considered a no-mans-land. You have to give props to these type of bold business owners, creative visionaries who are willing to to go where no man has gone before (sorry, couldn't resist). Not to get too smarmy, but this is what makes *Grand* pretty grand. Even though this place is not on a well-worn path, it is most certainly worth the trek because Wendy and Jon are the new mavens of Boston's shopping scene. Mark my words.

covet:
carve your own postcard
tovolo perfect ice cube tray
fee brothers bitters
binth alphabet
envirosax
roost glass water bottle
paddywax candles
acrylic tumblers

graymist studio & shop

a taste of the sea

364 huron avenue. between lake view and fayerweather. red line: harvard square
617.868.8688 www.graymiststudio.com
mon - sat 10a - 6p

opened in 2005. owner: etsuko yashiro
all major credit cards accepted
classes

west cambridge > 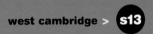 **s13**

It's been awhile since I set foot on an ocean beach, although it sort of felt like I did when I visited *GrayMist*. Etsuko makes the most intricately crafted Nantucket baskets, and what's even more wonderful is that she also teaches classes on this craft. If you're less than crafty, no worries, you can simply stick to shopping. You will find beachy items here that will make you want to throw a party at the seaside, or if that's not in the cards, a seashore-inspired soiree at your own home. Either way, *GrayMist* will inspire.

covet:
nantucket baskets
whale bone accent pieces
tagua nut accessories
seashell soap
wooden whale puzzle
wildflowers of maine
woven napkin rings

greenward

mod meets eco

1764 massachusetts avenue. between arlington and linnaean. red line: porter square
617.395.1338 www.greenwardshop.com
mon - wed 11a - 6p thu 11a - 8p fri - sat 11a - 6p sun noon - 5p

opened in 2007. owners: scott walker and simone alpen
all major credit cards accepted
online shopping

porter square > **s14**

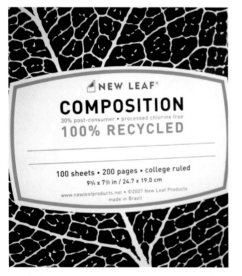

Finding clever ways to avoid pollution and waste can be satisfying. Making stock with vegetable ends; re-purposing tin cans; using coffee grinds in the garden. Beyond doing good for the planet, all these acts have an air of MacGyver coolness to them. *Greenward* is filled with cool things that brilliant, green-minded people have repurposed and reused, as well as items that will help you cut back on waste, like stainless steel water bottles and re-usable bags. Just try to tell me that this whole eco thing isn't loads of fun.

covet:
amenity modern organic placemats
twist loofah sponge
bambu kids fork & spoon
ecolution hemp washcloth
thames & kosmos wind power science kit
stainless steel straws
new leaf recycled composition book
taza organic chocolate

holiday

pretty little things

53 charles street. between mt. vernon and chestnut. red line: charles/mgh
617.973.9730 www.holidayboutique.net
mon - thu 11a - 7p fri 11a - 6p sat 10a - 6p sun noon - 5p

opened in 2002. owner: jessica pavlic
all major credit cards accepted
tailoring. private shopping parties

beacon hill > **s15**

Holidays. They always sound so appealing—a time to celebrate and have fun. Yet, I spent the last four holidays of note in a frenzy of cooking, cleaning, wrapping and gifting. Argh! Am I the only one who's experienced this? I think not. So, I'm heading to *Holiday*, the boutique, to have the kind of holiday I really need. Holiday martyrs, I'm inviting you to a place of celebration—where no one has to cook, clean or bake—and shopping is the gift that you give yourself!

covet:
loeffler randall
paul & joe
lauren moffatt
sunner
j brand
development
tory burch
signature holiday collection

hudson

dream home decor

312 shawmut avenue. between union park and waltham. orange line: back bay
617.292.0900 www.hudsonboston.com
mon - wed 10a - 6p thu 10a - 7p fri - sat 10a - 6p sun 11a - 5p

opened in 2006. owner: jill goldberg
all major credit cards accepted
registries. design services

south end > s16

In the past few years, while trying to find a new place to live, I have seen close to 100 different homes. It sounds fun to see how people live, open closets at will, and steal design ideas. But in reality, there are few ideas to steal out there, and most places look like the before picture in a reality home makeover show. I keep on hoping I'll see a place that is as stunning as *Hudson*. This place is motivation for beautifying my own home. My mantra: life is short, why waste it living without good design? Get to *Hudson* today and follow my teachings, you will thank me later.

covet:
dash & albert rugs
seda france candles
provence sante soaps
swans island blanket
iron spoons
vintage trunks
matteo bedding
vintage pillows

kitchenarts

a cook's essentials

215 newbury street. between exeter and fairfield. green line: copley
617.266.8701 www.kitchenarts.biz
mon - sat 10a - 7p sun 11a - 6p

opened in 1980. owner: owen mack
all major credit cards accepted
online shopping

back bay > **s17**

When's the last time you took a really good look inside your kitchen drawers? Using the same broken wooden spoon, the same dull knife, and the same crusty pot year after year? I think more often than not, our kitchens are affected by inertia, and so now is the time to take action and head to *KitchenArts*. Clear out the old stuff, and find yourself the right tools that will get you re-invigorated about cooking. Admit it, it's not satisfying to just throw something in the microwave, is it? No! So stop doing it, and re-discover the joy of actually using your kitchen to cook with the help of *KitchenArts*.

covet:
global knives
in-house knife sharpening
le creuset dutch oven
colorful colanders
wooden rolling pins
zyliss lobster crackers
stick-um candle adhesive
handyaid jar opener

137

koo de kir

interior design haven

65 chestnut street. corner of charles. red line: charles/mgh
617.723.8111 www.koodekir.com
mon - fri 11a - 7p sat 11a - 6p sun noon - 6p

opened in 1995. owner: kristine irving
all major credit cards accepted
online shopping. registries. design services

beacon hill > s18

I've been in mourning for months about the shuttering of one of my favorite shelter magazines, and wondering how I'm going to get my monthly dose of inspiration. But I think I have the solution: I'm going to go straight to the source. Just taking a circle through *Koo de Kir* gives me as many ideas as my favorite home design mags, and better yet, if I want see something firsthand, there it is right in front of me to peruse. If you're really in need of help, you can also hire Kristine to come over and make your home look as good as the pages of a magazine, or for that matter, *Koo de Kir*.

covet:
taika dinnerware
juliska glass cake plate
eva zeisel vases
nesting bowl set
jonas damon led clock
merriam-webster's thesaurus
elizabeth yarborough cashmere bangles
table stories charger

lekker

unique outfittings for life

1317 washington street. corner of waltham. orange line: back bay
617.542.6464 www.lekkerhome.com
tue - sat 10a - 7p sun noon - 6p

opened in 2003. owners: natalie van dijk carpenter and curt carpenter
all major credit cards accepted
online shopping

south end > **s19**

Why-oh-why would anyone register at big department store anymore—where scan guns are involved and attention to good design is often not—when there is a store like *Lekker* that can fulfill all your needs? Never fear, I'm here to spread the good word to not only those about to take their vows, but also to those who vow to fill their lives with good design. I suppose my desire to help is not entirely altruistic, as I would like to do all my gift shopping here, then I can pick out an item or two for my own home. In fact, I think I have an anniversary coming up that would be worthy of a *Lekker* gift. Hint hint.

covet:
royal copenhagen
arzberg containers
heath ceramics seasonal collection
stelton oil lamps
modern twist placemats
eva zeisel brass candlesticks
woodnotes newspaper stands
dwell studio bedding

lester harry's

designer clothing for babes and tots

115 newbury street. between clarendon and dartmouth. green line: copley
617.927.5400 www.lesterharrys.com
mon - sat 10a - 6p sun noon - 6p

opened in 2002. owner: jane seifert curley
all major credit cards accepted
online shopping. registries

back bay > **s20**

Judging from the photos in my baby album, *Lester Harry's* was not around when I was a baby. I can't complain about my hand-sewn, hand-knit ensembles, most of which were quite adorable. But I will say that if I had to go back and dress myself as an infant, I might turn to this place. With soft, stripy Splendid onesies, cool little numbers from Flora and Henri, and simple looks from Petit Bateau—I'm sold. Fellows, if you are looking for a manly onesie for your newborn emblazoned with "I'm a boob man," you must look elsewhere.

covet:
makié
superga
flora & henri
splendid
petit bateau
erbaviva
mustela
mini mella

looc

eye-catching style for women

12 union park street. between shawmut and washington. orange line: back bay
617.357.5333 www.loocboutique.com
tue - fri 11a - 7p sat 11a - 6p sun noon - 5p

opened in 2007. owner: audra boyle
all major credit cards accepted

south end > **s21**

There was always a girl in school, starting in the first grade, who looked perfect. All the time. Her ponytail had a pristine flip and an un-mussed bow; her class photo was never goofy or awkward. Years later in high school and college, that girl turned into the one whose style was impeccable, accessorizing in a seemingly effortless way. That girl now shops at *Looc*. I've never seen a more beautifully put-together store. Though I'm almost positive I'll never master the ponytail flip, I could definitely get used to shopping at *Looc*.

covet:
trovata
dress
steven alan
what goes around
lyell
lerario beatriz
alyssa norton
lizzie fortunato jewels

145

machine age

modern furniture and accessories

645 summer street. at pappas way. red line: south station
617.464.0099 www.machine-age.com
tue - sat noon - 4p and by appointment

opened in 1991. owner: normand mainville
all major credit cards accepted

fort point > **s22**

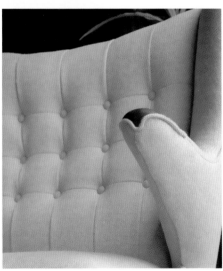

So much of the day I'm weighed down by modern machines: cell phone, digital camera, laptop, video camera, music player. Every once in awhile, I long for a day free of electronics—in fact, free of any type of machine. A day where I could just sit in a comfortable chaise lounge and read a good book. Since I don't have this piece of furniture, I would come to *Machine Age*, and browse the rows of classic pieces to pair with my classic novel. Unlike rapidly changing, rapidly obsolete electronic machinery, these pieces only get better and better with age.

covet:
charles eames executive time life chair
pepe cortes for knoll jamaica stool
1954 hans wegner daybed
borge mogensen settee
hans wegner teak dining table
geoge nelson folding dining table
eero saarinen table and chairs
george nelson side table with planter

147

matsu

style from across the globe

259 newbury street. between fairfield and gloucester. green line: copley
617.266.9707 www.matsuboston.com
mon - sat 11a - 6p sun 1 - 5p

opened in 1996. owner: dava muramatsu
all major credit cards accepted
consultation services

back bay > **s23**

Step into *Matsu*. Close your eyes. Inhale deeply. Where are you? Depending on the day, you might be traveling through India, or maybe wandering through Middle Eastern souks. Entering *Matsu* is like crossing over into a foreign land. Scarves from Italy, candles from France, music from Morocco. And your tour guide on this adventure will be Dava. She'll be your guru, sensei and shaman; your stylist and organizer. In short, she'll be your everything by leading you to the perfect piece of clothing or key accessory for making this journey extraordinary.

covet:
commes des garçon
lilith
inhabit
cotelac
rozae nichols
chan luu
jeanine payer
miller et bertaux

149

mdf / motto

artful pieces of jewelry and design

17-19 brattle street. at harvard square. red line: harvard square
mdf: 617.491.2789 / motto: 617.868.8448
mon - sat 10a - 6p sun noon - 6p

opened in 1980. owner: jude silver
all major credit cards accepted

harvard square > **s24**

Every year at Christmas, one of the highlights for the girls in my family is in the toe of our stockings. For in this tiny toe holds my dad's contribution to the holiday shopping of the year. Quite often what we find on Christmas morning is a beautiful and totally original piece of jewelry, for which my dad has a story about the place he found it, the designer who made it, and why he loved it. I'm fairly certain if he found himself at the two neighboring sister stores, *MDF* and *Motto*, he would be set with stocking gifts for years to come.

covet:
michael aram
aridza bross
japanese ceramics
jewelry:
   dori csengeri
   himat singka
   miguel ases
   terri logan

michelle willey

home accoutrements and design

8 union park street. between shawmut and washington. silver line: south end
617.424.6700 www.michellewilley.com
tue - sat 11a - 6p sun noon - 5p

opened in 2005. owner: michelle willey
all major credit cards accepted
registries

south end > s25

It's hard not to think that cleanliness is next to godliness while shopping at *Michelle Willey*—this is a heavenly place. I want to stock up on cleaning, kitchen and bath goods here, take them home and put them to use beautifying everything in sight. Painted white metal buckets, woven baskets for organization, canvas laundry baskets, beautiful dust brooms, linen aprons, and organic cotton flour sack cloths—Michelle's approach shows that a simple, clean and classic look will last you forever—and maybe put you that much closer to God in the meantime.

covet:
horsehair counter brush
cotton flour sack towels
red stripe cotton towel
matouk linens
beeswax candles
steele canvas totes & laundry baskets
apica notebooks
pigma micron pen

nest

a home and garden shop

875 main street. between columbia and cherry. red line: central square

617.354.0643

mon - sun 11a - 6p

opened in 2009. owners: gail and jean brooks

all major credit cards accepted

central square > 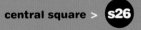 **s26**

Though a life in the country would be idyllic, there is something immensely satisfying about growing an urban garden. I love looking at all of the community gardens in Boston, where each plot of land is a thriving oasis, standing out green and vibrant against the steel and glass cityscape. To make an ideal city garden, come to *Nest*. It's full of items you'll want to incorporate into your growing, and home accessories that don't require a green thumb. *Nest* is a little slice of country respite smack in the middle of the city— your own little nest of nature.

covet:
positively green eco cards
vintage sprinkler heads
wooden birds
recycled glass vases
pover organic t's
ew studios market bags
antique wooden pull cart
vintage furniture

nomad

a traveler's findings

1741 massachusetts avenue. between prentiss and linnaean. red line: porter square
617.497.6677 www.nomadcambridge.com
mon - fri 10a - 7p sat 10a - 6p sun noon - 6p

opened in 1987. owner: deb colburn
all major credit cards accepted

porter square > s27

For those who love to shop the markets and small shops of a foreign country, nothing is as rewarding as finding a one-of-a-kind piece to carry home. Deb has created an entire store around this good feeling—*Nomad*. You can come explore the finds from her travels, or you can sign up to go along with her on one of her "Art and Soul" tours, where she takes a group to an exotic locale to visit artisans in their small villages, tour unusual markets and eat divine food. Whether you're a nomad here in this store or are one out there in the world, Deb will be there to guide you.

covet:
obama cloth & bag
jane diaz jewelry
afghan rings
thai plastic mats
silver milagros
seed bracelets
nava zahavi jewelry
art & soul tours

north river outfitter

preppy outfits for guys and gals

126 charles street. corner of revere. red line: charles/mgh
617.742.0089 www.northriveroutfitter.com
mon - thu 10a - 7p fri - sat 10a - 6p sun 11a - 5p

opened in 2007. owner: alice b. indelicato
all major credit cards accepted
online shopping

beacon hill >

There is a side of me that is helplessly preppy. It comes out at various times of the year (summer) and during certain sports (golf) and activities—like perusing *North River Outfitter*. I find myself going batty for Lily Pulitzer, all things seersucker and anything with an alligator on it. This store is a haven for those who believe monogramming is essential, headbands are timeless not trendy, and that a pair of pearl earrings really pulls you together. Gentlemen, you'll find your fair share of blazers, belts and boxer shorts here that fit the prepster bill as well.

covet:
alden shoes
lily pulitzer
vineyard vines
oyster belts
bill's khakis
smathers & branson
lacoste
custom built boats

passport

essentials for travel

43 brattle street. between brattle and church. red line: harvard square
617.576.0900 www.passportboutique.com
mon - thu 10:30a - 6p fri - sat 10:30a - 7p sun noon - 5p

opened in 2008. owner: jessica good
all major credit cards accepted

harvard square >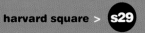

Glamour is not the first word that pops into my head when I think about travel. Frustration? Yes. Long lines? Uh-huh. Confusion? Absolutely. *Passport* is here to change these associations, giving travel back a sense of enjoyment and a touch of style from the days of old. Cashmere wrap? Check. Lavender-infused hand wipes? Check. A pretty silver passport cover? Check. Luggage that doesn't look like you're packing for your own funeral? Check. Any other transportation need you might have, check in with owner Jessica, she's probably got a solution for it.

covet:
tepper jackson luggage tags
the laundress travel set
herban essentials
marimekko umbrellas
twinkle zip belts
white + warren slippers
love ya-ya dress
passport wallets

pod

textiles and treats for you and your home

313 washington street. between harvard and school. green line d: brookline village
617.739.3802 www.shop-pod.com
see website for hours

opened in 1998. owner: julie baine
all major credit cards accepted
online shopping

brookline >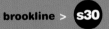

When I was little, on occasion I would set up camp and sleep in my closet. The closet was a perfect square, so one side held my makeshift bed, the other held all of my favorite, most prized possessions I couldn't leave behind in my room. I loved being in that closet, it was my own little pod, an edited selection of my life. I couldn't help but have that same feeling when I came to *Pod*, which is Julie's own little perfectly edited world. Miraculously, what she carries fits perfectly into what I'd take with me to my closet these days—including a beautiful new soft blanket to sleep with.

covet:
regina barrios jewelry
ethiopian scarves
makie dress
gold tessa clogs
fog linens
lucia soaps
area blankets
d.u.e. by matteo

polka dog bakery

a bakery and boutique for dogs

256 shawmut avenue. corner of milford. orange line: back bay
617.338.5155 www.polkadog.com
mon - fri 10a - 7:30p sat 10a - 7p sun 10a - 6p

opened in 2002. owner: robert van sickle
all major credit cards accepted
online shopping

south end > **s31**

While wandering around the South End, you might pass a ball park, where on just about sunny day you'll see dogs galloping about, looking loopily happy. You might reason that it's the sunshine and outdoor play that have made these pups joyous, but you'd be partially wrong. Just a block away is *Polka Dog Bakery* where, more than likely, their owners have just treated them to a tasty pig's ear or a fresh-from-the-bakery peanut butter bar. If I were a canine with a bakery like this in my town, I'd be pretty dog-gone happy too.

covet:
polkadog packabowl
bubba's beef box
chicken littles
treatza pizza
chicken kung pug
tuna yelper
liver's lane
bag of bones

proletariat

skate and art supply and more

36 jfk street, #2-27b. corner of mt. auburn. red line: harvard square
617.661.3865 www.proletariatboston.com
mon - sat noon - 8p sun noon - 6p

opened in 2004. owner: kerry simon
all major credit cards accepted
online shopping

harvard square > **s32**

Lest you think that graffiti is not actually a true form of art, I ask you to check out the work of artist Shepard Fairey—genius street artist and muralist who had his beginnings as a rogue, underground prankster. These days his work is exhibited at ICA, and he is world famous for his Obama campaign posters. If you're not interested in playing by the rules, *Proletariat* is your type of joint. Here you can pick up graffiti supplies, some clothing if you're into wearing any, and a skateboard for when you need a quick get-away.

covet:
proletariat hoverboard
america tote bag
vintage harvard sweater
a revolt t's
378 raw denim
kingpen opaque paint markers
spraypaint
tips

reside

classic mid-century modern

266 concord avenue. corner of appleton. red line: harvard square

617.547.2929 www.resideinc.com

mon noon - 6p tue - sat 10a - 6p sun noon - 6p

opened in 2002. owner: pamela watts

all major credit cards accepted

online shopping

west cambridge > **s33**

I have trouble sitting still. I'm always running around, finding something to keep me busy, rarely relaxing. Part of the problem is that I haven't found a seat comfortable enough to keep me in one place long enough to relax in. *Reside* is full of chairs and sofas that I think I could actually kick back in, relax for awhile. And on a happy side note, it's a given that anything from *Reside* is going to be incredibly good-looking—there is no sacrificing style for some lazy-boy livin'.

covet:
wood african passports
rosewood credenza
amorphous coffee table
vintage cribbage board
danish teak high back chair
teak trays
florence knoll credenza
hans brattrud rosewood lounge chair

salmagundi

fine hats

765 centre street. between eliot and burroughs
617.522.5047 www.salmagundiboston.com
tue - sat 11a - 8p sun 10a - 6p

opened in 2007. owners: andria rapagnola and jessen fitzpatrick
mc. visa

jamaica plain >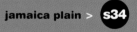

Some say JFK is to blame for hats going out of style. He was always hatless, showcasing that extraordinary head of hair. It's taken a long time, but men'shats are finally back. I am happy for the hats' return, as are many men, who can now buy their lids at *Salmagundi*. There's styles a-plenty to choose from here, plus other men's accessories and lovelies for the ladies as well. And a suggestion for hat wearing men: there's a fine line between the smart style of *Mad Men* and K-Fed trashiness. Stay sharp to stay cool.

covet:
peter grimm straw hats
scala sun hat
block headwear hats
kangol hats
p.f. flyers silver shoes
bailey of hollywood hats
eight sixty black & white dress

shake the tree

gifts and more

67 salem street. between cross and parmenter
orange / green lines: haymarket street
617.742.0484 www.shakethetreeboston.com
see website for hours

opened in 1994. owner: marian l. klausner
all major credit cards accepted

north end > **s35**

Long ago my mom was so hard-pressed to find a last-minute gift that she re-gifted a frame we had, wrapping it up and making it look like new. Problem solved, crisis averted! Wrong-o. In her haste, she'd forgotten to remove the family photo, thus outing herself and her lousy re-gifting strategies to the receiver. To avoid any similar disasters, there is no need to shake up the house looking for a present, you can come to *Shake the Tree*, where all gift giving problems can and will be solved and embarrassing catastrophes avoided.

covet:
pantone mugs
orla kiely wallets
carte postale postcards
vosges chocolate
ame & lulu zip wallets
banho bath soap
moroccan shot glasses
bellisimi cuffs

simplemente blanco

460 harrison avenue, #b15. corner of thayer. silver line: east berkeley
617.734.3669 www.simplementeblanco.com
by appointment only

opened in 2004. owner: fernanda bourlot
all major credit cards accepted
custom orders/design

south end > **s36**

GARDEN

I recently packed up everything I owned in a matter of weeks to get ready for the fastest move ever. As I was pulling my belongings out of every nook, and looking at the mish-mash of stuff, I thought to myself that I would like to simplify. *Simplemente Blanco* came to mind. This calming space is filled with hand-crafted materials and could serve as my inspiration for a fresh start. It doesn't take a move to start over though, so give Fernanda a ring to make an appointment, and allow her to inspire a clean new look for your own home.

covet:
pillows
napkin rings
soaps
bags
curtains
garden tools carrier
bulbs
men's toiletries

175

stel's

classic style with an edge for men and women

334 newbury street. between massachusetts and hereford
green line: hynes convention center
617.262.3348 www.stelsinc.com
mon - fri 11a - 7p sat 11a - 8p sun noon - 6p

opened in 2004. owners: tina burgos, john callahan and dave nauyokas
all major credit cards accepted
online shopping

back bay > **s37**

As a freelancer who works from home, I get a little lazy when it comes to getting "dressed for work." When the need arises to make a run for printer paper, I often find myself in the streets looking like a wreck. It's at these times that I realize I need a uniform. A classic yet interesting outfit that is comfy enough for hunkering down in, yet stylish enough to be seen out in the world. *Stel's* is my dream shop to buy said uniform. Here's what I would pick: a Rachel Comey scarf, Rogan jeans and a long Alexander Wang tank. Now i've got to get back to work so I can support my shopping needs.

covet:
robert geller
nom de guerre
apc
rogan
coven
alexander wang
gary graham
angel jackson

tadpole

modern goods for modern kids

toys: 37 clarendon street. corner of gray. orange line: back bay
gear: 58 clarendon street. corner of chandler. orange line: back bay
617.778.1788 www.shoptadpole.com
tue - fri 10a - 7p sat 10a - 6p sun noon - 5p

opened in 2006. owners: david hauck and storey heironymous hauck
all major credit cards accepted
online shopping. registries. kids events

south end > **s38**

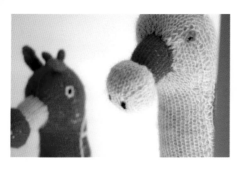

A few years ago, everyone around me was getting married. Now, everyone around me is having a baby, so much so that I can barely keep up with all of the gift buying. Lucky friends, you've all picked a pretty good time to have a kid, as I'm heading to *Tadpole* to buy you and your future offspring presents! This is exactly where I want to do my gift-buying business, as the two stores are filled with well-designed modern items ranging from groovy Bumbleride strollers to Boon squirt spoons. So go forth and multiply, *Tadpole* and I will keep you properly outfitted.

covet:
uppababy strollers
skip*hop everything
boon snackball
sprig recycled trucks
auto moblox
plan toys alligator
pink chicken clothing
green to grow bottle

the beauty mark

a cosmetics and beauty boutique

33 charles street. between chestnut and mt. vernon. red line: charles/mgh
617.720.1555 www.thebeautymark.com
mon - fri 11a - 7p sat 10a - 6p sun noon - 5p

opened in 2003. owner: amy bailey
all major credit cards accepted
beauty services

beacon hill >  **s39**

As someone who has lots of "beauty marks" spotted all over my face—I can tell you that, whoever deemed a brown mole a thing of beauty was pretty darn good at marketing. Then there's the lovely cosmetics boutique *Beauty Mark* that is very good at making ladies pretty, from beautifying your feet (you can come here for a quick pedicure) to applying make up that enhances, not hides your features. And there are cosmetics galore to choose from. You won't need a marketer to persuade you that this store is truly a place of beauty.

covet:
model co.
kai
lipstick queen
duwop
le charche midi
bumble & bumble
skinceuticals
l'annine

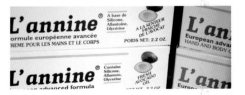

181

twentieth century limited

vintage designer costume jewelry

73 charles street. betwen pinckney and mt. vernon. red line: charles/mgh
617.742.1031 www.boston-vintagejewelry.com
mon - sat 11a - 6p sun noon - 5p

opened in 1995. owner: paul turnberg
all major credit cards accepted

beacon hill > **s40**

My mom taught me what her mom taught her: never throw away jewelry. This means any kind, since you never know when, a) it might be in style again, b) there might be serious demand for it or, c) when you might be able to rework it. Thankfully, not everyone recieved the same advice, allowing Paul to amass the most impressive collection of vintage designer jewelry that I've seen at *Twentieth Century Limited*. If you do find an amazing piece here, the remember the advice I was given and hold on to your new "old" gem forever.

covet:
mirriam haskell
trifari
schiaparelli
juliana
weiss
liz nania
hobé
bakelite

urban living studio

urbane goods for uban living

535 albany street, studio 3a. corner of wareham. orange line: back bay
617.717.6805 www.urbanlivingstudio.com
by appointment only

opened in 2007. owner: kristen gaughan
all major credit cards accepted
design services

south end > **s41**

I spend a lot of time in my home office, so it's important to have an inspiring space to enhance productivity. Or to be truthful, to provide a good space to dilly-dally and procrastinate. I can picture my home in a manner that Kristen from *Urban Living Studio* would design it. She might suggest I make my bed with Area Bedding, which is a good reason to never leave my bed for my home office—i will have a bed office. Now that *Urban Living* has transitioned from a traditional storefront to more of a studio environment, Kristen can offer interior design services and she will still offer some of her favorite product lines. Brilliant.

covet:
oil cloth bags
ruff studio recycled banner totoe
color block 2-tone tote
niho kozuru beeswax candles
thomas paul print pillows
area bedding
iittala glassware
chilewich place mats

185

vessel

smart designer goods

125 kingston street. between essex and beach. orange line: chinatown
877.805.1801 www.vessel.com
tue - sat 11a - 6p sun noon - 5p

opened in 2005. owner: stefane barbeau and duane smith
all major credit cards accepted
online shopping

chinatown >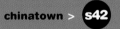

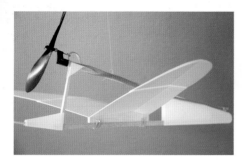

I'm sort of tempted to steal a piece of the mission statement *Vessel* has printed on the wall of their store: "we feature designs by like-minded companies that we feel are worthy of a spot in everyone's life." This reads like a part of the *eat.shop* motto. In a world full of bad design (Beanie Babies and Crocs for example), we advocate that consumers spend their dollars locally and on good design, like *Vessel's*. Everything here, whether it be a *Vessel* product or one of their compatriot's products, is appealing, smart, and useful. *eat.shop* + *Vessel* = love.

covet:
vessel:
  hippietipi
  eiko egg boilers
  simha knives
  candela lights
  tempo tags
kuvert bags
malin+goetz